TALK LESS AND SHOW MORE

Carol,
Thanks for
being a champion
for children.

Dr. Ahwa

TALK LESS AND SHOW MORE

16 PROFESSIONAL LEARNING STRATEGIES
THAT MAKE CONTENT STICK

Shera Carter Sackey, PhD

Talk Less and Show More: 16 Professional Learning Strategies That Make Learning Stick

For special orders, quantity sales, course adoptions, and corporate sales, please email us at sales@drsherasackey.com

Published by: Education Empowerment Zone Press

ISBN-13: 9781544037271
ISBN: 1544037279
Library of Congress Control Number: 2017917051

Printed in the United States of America.

CONTENTS

Acknowledgements

How was the last professional development session you attended? Was it energizing and engaging? Or, was it boring and mundane? Recently, I participated in a professional learning session on learner-centered teaching. About an hour into the session, I felt my eyes glaze over, and I struggled to focus. I felt like I was in a professional development prison. There was limited peer-to-peer interaction in what seemed to be one long, never-ending lecture. I certainly did not want to be negative, so I plastered a smile on my face. Here is the bottom line: the topic of this workshop was learner-centered teaching, yet this session felt like the exact opposite. Over the course of the session, there was limited interaction, movement, discussion, and other brain-based strategies that promote active learning.

For more than 15 years, I have presented to adult audiences. Consequently, this resource is dedicated to people who teach, train, and deliver presentations and want to go from telling and talking to showing and transforming.

I want to acknowledge education consultants, speakers, and authors who walk their talk, such as Shirley Hord, Joellen Killion, Juwanza Kunjufu, Eric Jensen, Kim McCleod, Aric Bostick, Carol Francois, Stephanie Hirsh, Marcia Tate, Terri Morganti-Fisher, Jenice Pizzuto, and Deborah Hunter-Harvill. They remind us that it is important to present and facilitate adult and student learning that leads to significant change. They remind us that learning should be job-embedded and continuous.

They also remind us that titles and credentials are important; however, people crave connection.

I also acknowledge those corporate, K-12, and collegiate learning environments that show and model learning that is engaging, relevant, and meaningful. In these environments, data drives decision making, and collaboration is fostered in communities of learning that are reflective and adaptive.

I'm thankful for my family, who encourages me to dream bigger and speak boldly, even when my voice is shaky. I am thankful to Learning Forward for hiring me to consult with principals, school leaders, and teachers, both nationally and internationally. Thank you, Shanedria Wagner, my editor, for your continued support and inspiration.

ABOUT THE AUTHOR

What I've Learned in Fifteen Years

I am the founder of Education Empowerment Zone, an organization geared toward helping individuals and organizations to optimize learning and communication in order to maximize results. I am a keynote speaker, educational consultant, experienced trainer, published author, and college professor, having served in many educational roles including staff developer, campus administrator, and classroom teacher. I have also conducted corporate communication skills training, helped scores of K-12 school leaders implement professional learning communities, and assisted others to transform into excellent presenters and trainers. I've always been captivated with the process of developing fun and engaging learning opportunities that also change mindsets and actions that ultimately lead to achieving individual and organizational goals. As I voraciously read, research, learn, and teach, I continue to challenge myself to simplify the process of offering relevant, meaningful high-quality instruction to both children and adults. A culmination of the results is in this resource. Use, reference, and apply it to achieve your goals of learning success for both educators and students.

You Won't Just Know How to ACHIEVE—You WILL Leverage It

This method facilitates teaching since it distills the essential elements of lesson planning/instructional design and best practices in learning and presenting, which enables one to teach and train effectively in face-to-face and online learning environments. You will practice and rehearse what you cultivate, so when you teach or train, you will be prepared.

Who is this for?

I have taught countless people how to successfully leverage learning by employing best practices, in varied contexts, including face-to-face training and coaching in virtual environments. Superintendents utilize these skills to leverage organizational learning. District office personnel use this method to strengthen employee skills. Principals employ these skills to ensure that teachers are engaged in high-quality learning that drives student achievement, and teacher-leaders utilize them to structure and deliver engaging lessons for diverse students.

Success

I am certain that using these methods will assist you with garnering success as you define it, so I want to recognize you. Please email your success stories to drshera@drsherasackey.com and in the subject field write ACHIEVE Success. We want to celebrate your successes, add you or your organization to our "Success Hall of Fame," and provide you with a gift.

ABOUT THIS BOOK

Although one will find a variety of books that focus on professional learning and development, instructional design/lesson planning, training, or presentation skills, rarely does one find a book that closes the gaps by focusing on leading and mastering these initiatives. This text also helps school leaders and staff developers garner more social currency through the use of effective communication skills. This book integrates academic research, but it is also practical and purposely brief enough to fit into a briefcase.

This book, which is organized into sections, is replete with immediately implementable strategies. You will learn techniques for using data to identify areas of focus. You will determine the best types of learning intervention to achieve (and surpass) your goals. You will focus on engagement and why subject-matter expertise is not sufficient to effectively reach and teach adult and young learners. You will also learn how to participate in a cycle of continuous improvement by monitoring and assessing the quality of instruction and delivery modalities. This book provides step-by-step guidance to develop engaging, high-yield professional learning that includes checklists, templates, worksheets, and additional resources to ensure you achieve, leverage learning, and obtain success as you define it. The information provides the tools you need to provide high-quality instruction in face-to-face and virtual environments. This book focuses primarily on those who lead and provide training to district-level and school-based employees.

Online Templates and Additional Resources
Additionally, I have included the checklists, templates, and worksheets you need to create a dynamic class. I have also created a special part of the website exclusively for you. By visiting www.drsherasackey.com, you may download select templates, checklists, and worksheets in this book, plus additional resources. This will enable you to design training or a class on various topics.

A Quick Guide to the Achieve Method Terms
ACHIEVE: A four-step instructional design, delivery, and evaluation process for job-embedded professional learning. The four steps include the following: Content, Organization, Delivery, and Evaluation. Content includes the organization/individual goals and what is taught, organization includes process and interventions, delivery is presentation skills, and evaluation is formative and summative assessment and feedback.

Continuous improvement: A constant search for a better way and a persistent discomfort with the status quo (DuFour & Eaker, 1998).

Face-to-face instruction: A learning environment that takes place formally or informally where the learners are physically present.

Leader: A person who is self-directed, exercises personal responsibility, and positively influences himself and others to achieve individual and organizational goals, using effective communication techniques and best practices in training, teaching, and learning.

Leadership: Refers to "the state of having influence over people and events, whether through a formal position or informal status to achieve desired outcomes" (Peppers, 2014, p. 15).

Learning organization: "An organization that is continually expanding its capacity to create its future" (Senge, 1990, p. 14).

Virtual Learning: Learning that occurs formally or informally in mediated formats.

My Learning Outcomes for You

By reading this book and completing the activities, you will be able to do the following:

- Identify and prioritize the most important learning gaps based on organizational or classroom goals.
- Determine whether training is the best way to address performance-based issues that impede student achievement.
- Determine the best way to address learning gaps in your organization or classroom.
- Build the framework for an effective course.
- Evaluate the course's impact.
- Use appropriate methods to design effective courses.
- Apply effective techniques for compelling conversations.
- Practice techniques for delivering effective presentations.

So, let's get started!

STRATEGY #1

MAKE IT RELEVANT
What's in It for You: Why Optimized Learning?

Significant learning results in change.
—*D.L. FINK*

- Are you a school leader who must provide high-quality staff development for increased teacher or student outcomes?
- Has your supervisor asked you to develop training on a specialized topic?
- Are you an instructor who wants to maximize participant learning?
- Do you have to provide staff development for a lot of people with a limited amount of time?
- Do budget constraints impact the type of staff development provided?
- Are you tempted to quickly create a slide show, hoping the learning sticks?

There is a faster, powerful, results-driven way!

Convert your expertise, or the expertise of those you lead, into engaging, effective, inspirational learning sessions using the Achieve Method. The Achieve Method provides you with the skills you need to go beyond "Sit and Get" to create and launch high-quality learning, provide powerful educational opportunities, and leverage the expertise in the organization. When I first started teaching and attending professional development workshops, I soon began to dread the boring, laborious, "important" sessions. I heard a plethora of theory and data-driven research that was oftentimes confusing, and the training was delivered in a monotonous fashion. We were required to differentiate or provide personalized learning in our classrooms, yet these very "strategies" were not modeled in our trainings. Did the presenters not notice that the attendees' eyes were glazed over? After I became a campus-based staff developer, I realized that developing and presenting professional learning was a bit more challenging than it appeared. Could I make it entertaining, yet substantive? Could I make it relevant and meaningful? Would I hold the audience's attention? Would the participants actually learn and apply the concepts? Would my training impact their job performance?

Why does this matter?

With a significant emphasis on standards-based education and accountability, teacher practice has been under a microscope (Jones, Stall, & Yarbrough, 2013). According to Varela (2012), teachers have reported that professional development opportunities are usually isolated, passive, and provide limited engagement for participants. The new form of staff development that has emerged is one that is job-embedded, standards-driven, and results-based (Hirsh & Killion, 2007).

The Every Child Achieves Act of 2015 is sure to bring about much needed change to the educational landscape. The bill provides resources to states and school districts to implement various activities to support teachers, principals, and other educators, including allowable uses of funds for high-quality induction programs for new teachers, ongoing professional development opportunities for teachers, and programs to recruit new educators. Although states have more flexibility than ever, there will still be a focus on increasing student achievement among subpopulations. Recent education policy has significantly changed teaching and learning in the United States (Harris, 2011). These school reforms have integrated various innovations, such as conceptualizing schools as learning organizations with a focus on continuous improvement. This has led to school reform initiatives such as PLCs. The core mission of a PLC is to ensure that students learn, to establish a culture of collaboration, and to be focused on results (DuFour, 2004).

This model of school reform also focuses on what students have learned versus what they have been taught; the conceptualization of the school as a learning organization helps to navigate the age of accountability with an ongoing process through which teachers and administrators work collaboratively to seek and share learning and to act on their learning, their goal being to enhance their effectiveness as professionals for students' benefit (Hord, 1997).

It is vital that schools and districts become learning organizations in order to ensure that every student achieves. In order for this to happen, school and organizational leaders must lead the learning for effective professional learning. Professional development has been used as a school improvement option to change teacher practices and increase student outcomes (Burke, 2013).

What is optimized learning?

Optimized learning is significant learning that results in individual and organizational change. When individuals change, their practices change, and when practice changes, results are obtained. Optimized learning is predicated by shifts in mindset, skill, application, and evaluation.

Optimized Learning = Results

Achieve Method

1. Content: What do you want the participants to know?
2. Organization: How will you organize the content when facilitating a training session or giving a presentation?
3. Delivery: What is the best method of training to ensure optimal success?
4. Evaluation: How will the learning be evaluated?

Jump-Start Actions for *Learner-Centered Professional Development*
Let's get interactive! Jump-start your neurons as you explore the content in this book. Consider completing one or more of these activities to jump-start your learning.

1. Select two books based on brain-based learning, organizational learning, presentations, or training that you have previously read. What are similarities and differences? Discuss your findings with a colleague.
2. Quick write: Take two minutes to brainstorm and generate a list of the most effective ways to foster learning. Revisit this list to decide if you would like to revise it in any way.
3. What *Aha*s have you had about teaching and learning related to children or adults? What things have you come across that you completely disagree with?
4. Complete a short internet search about active learning. Make note of the websites that you might like to explore further.
5. How do you define communication? How do experts define it? Just because you are communicating, does that mean you are connecting?

STRATEGY #2

LEVERAGE LEADERSHIP
Leaders as Teachers, Trainers, and Facilitators

L eadership is integral to navigating organizational change. To become successful, or to sustain success, an organization must strengthen leadership. Leaders know that continuous improvement in curriculum, instruction, and systems require ongoing, high-quality professional learning (Standards of Professional Learning, 2011). Cultivating leaders that value learning and promote continuous improvement can help organizations easily adapt to rapidly changing environments.

In *Leading Change* by John Kotter, Kotter (2012) asserts that organizations that fail to change allow the following:

- Complacency
- Underestimation of the power of vision
- Barriers to impede success
- Absence of short-term wins
- Declarations of victory too soon
- Neglect to anchor change within the organizational culture

Leading effective school districts and schools entails promoting organizational and individual learning that garners results. What are some issues within your organization that need to be addressed? What knowledge, skills, and attitudes are needed that lead to performance improvement? How will you celebrate success?

Leaders as Teachers

Ed Ludwig, CEO of Beckton, Dickinson, and Co (BD), made some da-ta-driven changes. The data indicated, "That not everyone knew where they were going on the team." Although this data was relative to this company, there are many teachers, teacher-leaders, and other educa-tional stakeholders, who don't have a sense of mission, fully understand the organizational vision, or actualize their potential according to the systems that are in place. In the aforementioned scenario, Betof (2009) finds that BD learned they needed improved organizational learning processes, and they needed to dedicate more resources to talent man-agement and associate and leadership development to remain viable.

Betof (2009) also found that after developing the *leaders as teachers* program, these key elements stood out:

- Leaders as teachers, aligned with the organizations goals, can significantly improve performance.
- Leveraging talent within the organizations is more economical than hiring subject-matter experts and consultants.
- Leaders should expect resistance and/or conflict and deal with it proactively by creating positive buzz, celebrating wins, and fo-cusing on short-term success that builds momentum and leads to long-term results.
- Leaders should develop leadership in the organization, regard-less of position, and facilitate informal and formal learning op-portunities. Leaders should help others to identify and cultivate their talents and provide them with opportunities to collaborate with others and teach others. This will enable them to be more confident, enthusiastic, and effective.

This supports Learning Forward's finding that if increased student achievement is the goal, we must improve teacher practices, which is best achieved through professional learning.

STRATEGY #3

DETERMINE THE FOCUS FOR LEARNING

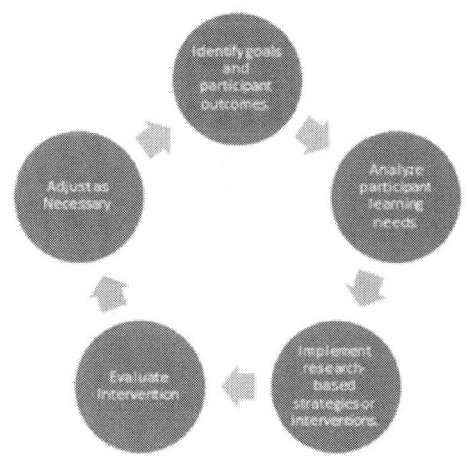

Select the Content: Identify Organizational Goals

Successful professional development is a blend of experiences that "empowers (a) individual educators, (b) educational teams, and (c) the educational organization to improve (d) curriculum, (e) instruction, and (f) student assessment in order to (g) facilitate student growth and development" (Gordon, 2004, p. 5). School improvement is necessary for an increase in student outcomes. Not all change leads to school improvement; however, school improvement does not take place without change (Gordon, 2004). Significant learning is learning that results in lasting change (Fink & Fink, 2009). It is very important to begin with the end in mind.

Achieve Method for Identifying Organizational Goals

Here is the 4-Step Process to help you identify the most important areas of focus. Goals should be specific, measurable, actionable, time-bound, and results oriented.

Step 1: Get Ready

1. What do you want to achieve?

2. What is happening that you don't want to happen?

3. What is most important? What are the top three priorities?

4. Where would you like to see the organization within the next five years?

Step 2: Set Your Goals

5. If you did not pursue anything else, what three things would make this year a success?

6. Why do you pursue this goal, and what are the benefits of achieving it?

7. When will you have achieved it?

8. How will you know you have achieved it? Identify the criteria for evidence of success.

9. How will you celebrate your wins?

Step 3: Implement Your Goals

10. What action(s) will you complete within the next 7 days?

11. Who are the team's cheerleaders? Who are the most influential and/or respected people in the organization (regardless of their titles)? How can you achieve buy-in from them? How could you engage them to support these goals and influence others? How could you engage skeptics?

12. What can we start and stop doing immediately to help us achieve our goals?

13. What are potential obstacles? If we were to sabotage ourselves, how could we do it?

14. What is the one thing that you can do right now that would have the most impact?

Step 4: On-Target

15. If you were to rate how likely you are to achieve these goals on a scale of 1–10, what would you rate yourself? ___/10
If you don't score at least an "8," you do not have a plan.

16. If your score is less than an "8," ask what you haven't mentioned, and explore the obstacles again while brainstorming solutions.

17. How will you celebrate improvement, progress, and completion?

Develop the Purpose for Learning

A learning outcome concretely describes what participants will be able to do that they haven't done before. Develop the purpose of the learning and then the outcome associated with it.

Developing the Purpose

The purpose of this class is to develop a program that addresses:

1. Action
2. Audience
3. Topic

You can interchange them, if necessary. It should be simple, realistic, and direct.

Examples

- The purpose of this two-hour session is to orient faculty and staff to Learning Forward's Standards of Professional Learning.
- The purpose of this 60-minute webinar is to teach you how to integrate two new active learning strategies this school year.
- Professional Learning Purpose.
- An essential element to the purpose statement is to highlight the benefits to the participants. This helps to make the topic relevant and significant. It also helps with audience interest and engagement.
- Compare the examples: Which ones are most desirable?

Before

- The purpose of this two-hour session is to orient Department Chairs to Learning Forward's Standards of Professional Learning.

After

- The purpose of this two-hour session is to help department chairs understand the standards for professional learning to foster job-embedded knowledge, skills, and practices that provide solutions to everyday subject-matter challenges.

Achieve Method—Putting it All Together

Content

Learning Objective: *What is the purpose/content that needs to be taught?*

To develop ways to foster student engagement.

Evidence: *What data informs this decision?*

In a recent discussion with faculty and staff, the staff reported that students seem to be disengaged and disinterested in learning the content.

Significance/Relevance: WIIFM (What's in it for me)? Why is it important for the learners to know? How can you create buy-in?

This is important because students need to listen and pay attention in order to learn.

Attention Getter: How will you open the training to galvanize participants to get involved? Will you ask a thought-provoking question, make a startling statement, use witty humor, show a video or movie clip, or state a profound quotation?

Opening: Ask the participants to recall times when they were engaged and disengaged in a class. Have each participant create a t-chart on paper to list characteristics of both engaging and disengaging lessons. After they have jotted these things down, ask each to find a shoulder partner to share.

Organization

How will it be structured? Select two items to focus on in order to "chunk the content" and deliver just-in time learning that participants can immediately implement.

Topic: Student Engagement

Activities: Discuss a collective definition of student engagement and review videos of classroom instruction from a different school to determine what student engagement is and is not.

Have participants break into small groups to discuss/record themes based on the observational data.

Topic: Student Engagement in Action

Activities: Have participants read an article on various student engagement strategies. Then have them select and incorporate a strategy in a 5-minute mini lesson that they will demonstrate in their small groups.

Delivery

How will you deliver the lesson? Can it be changed and delivered in an online format? Will you record the session if it is face-to-face? How will you obtain feedback on your oral and non-oral delivery? Is a training session needed for the issue or could a checklist be created? How will time be maximized?

I will present this lesson face-to-face, record it, and place it in a professional development repository for those who could not attend. I will use a survey to solicit feedback on my oral and non-oral delivery.

Evaluation

Assessment: Have teachers select one strategy to implement and include in their lesson plans. Have volunteers record and share their lessons with other teachers. Discuss what worked well and what did not. Create a follow-up survey and identify any trends in the data.

Celebration: Acknowledge the teachers who were willing to showcase their work with an announcement, recognition, or raffle, for example. Brainstorm to identify other gestures of appreciation for their willingness to show their work.

STRATEGY #4

KEEP THE AUDIENCE IN MIND

Analyzing the Audience

I n order for participants to be engaged in the learning, they have to perceive that they are receiving some benefit from participating in the learning. There has to be some buy-in or relevance. That is why it is so important to understand who my audience is. Audience analysis takes age, sex, gender, race, sexual orientation, religious affiliation, national origin, psychological characteristics, personality, educational background, group affiliations, and environmental characteristics into account. Why does this matter? You can provide a training session or presentation to one audience that receives rave reviews. You can provide the exact training to a completely different audience that does not go over well. What was the difference? The audience. This is significant, especially regarding some of your participants' frame of reference. Frame of reference takes into account the audience's background and experiences (Hamilton, 2014). A school leader has a different frame of reference than a person not in a leadership position. Yet, having a bird's eye view and a worm's eye view are equally important. Are your participants mostly millennials or baby boomers? This is significant regarding how they may perceive you or the topic.

When I became a Title 1 coordinator, I was very young. There were some teachers who were initially dismissive of my role since, according to them, I was "just a baby" and "still wet behind the ears." One teacher had the temerity to tell me that since she had been teaching for 20 years, I couldn't tell her anything. So in situations like these—in which collaboration is needed—it is important to build trust. Culture plays a significant factor too. Does being a person of color automatically mean that one uses culturally relevant teaching strategies? Dr. Jwanza Kunjufu, a leading researcher and author who specializes in cultural proficiency, would argue that it doesn't. The world is very diverse and complex, and the reactions you have to even the topic could vary based on the audience's attitudes, values, and belief systems, especially when it comes to topics that deal with race, culturally relevant teaching, gender issues, socio-economic issues, religion, and sexual orientation.

I'll never forget a time when I taught high school, and the school began a Gay Straight Alliance. This was before attitudes evolved regarding same-sex relationships. I remember this topic eliciting such passionate responses from teachers. If you are facilitating a session that is controversial, you have to demonstrate the significance of the topic, how it affects staff and students, and why there is a need for the change. One of the best ways to do this is through the use of supporting materials or evidence. One could use relevant examples, reliable statistics, expert testimony, emotional appeal, and logic and reason to illustrate how the change will benefit the students.

Other factors may be taken into account such as time of day, location, etc. If presenting after lunch, what will you do to energize the audience? If they have been learning something all day, have you allocated time for processing and reflection? How will you integrate active learning? Location matters: a training held in the cafeteria or gym may be received differently than a training held in a library or classroom. Are the acoustics good? Are the chairs comfortable? Is the screen large enough so that everyone can see? Environmental characteristics include expectations about the time, setting, and occasion.

What does personality have to do with anything?

Is your audience mostly extroverted, introverted, or ambiverted? Is there an even distribution? I taught a class recently where I pulled out an arsenal of engaging strategies, but nothing seemed to work. I could've stood on my head and not received a response. I started dreading going to the class. There was little to no engagement and I couldn't, for the life of me, figure out what was going wrong. Then, I began teaching self-awareness and administered the Jung Typology. As it turned out, most of them were introverts. As a result of discovering this vital information, I was able to adjust and engage with them differently.

The research overwhelmingly contends that tailoring your presentation to your audience is critical for success (Sellnow, 2005, Lucas, 2014). The experiences of your audience can influence their attitudes about your topic. If you want your message to succeed or for people to even have a desire to listen, you must acknowledge what they care about. Through audience analysis you can determine how your audience's beliefs are similar to and different from your own. You can adapt the presentation to demonstrate respect for various perspectives. The goal is to realize that more often than not, the audience will be demographically diverse. Even if there are those in an audience who share predominate characteristics, it is important to avoid stereotypes or assume too much about a particular demographic. Psychological characteristics include what motivates people to listen and retain the ideas. People are more motivated to listen if they can ascertain how they can benefit from the information. Telling participants there are benefits does not guarantee that they will perceive the message as beneficial. Have your parents ever told you to eat something that you didn't like because it was good for you? Conversely, avoiding topics that make people uncomfortable is not always advantageous. Reflect on the times that you have experienced the most growth in your life. Were you comfortable? Probably not. So, the instructor and the material to be taught have responsibilities that must be met with the audience regarding the learning.

What's in it for Me (WIIFM)

Most participants are interested in the "what's in it for me." These are questions they may ask, and I call these questions the Essential 6:

1. Why do I need to know this?
2. What do I need to do?
3. How will I do it?
4. How will I know if it is done right?
5. What can I do to improve?
6. How will success be acknowledged?

The content that is taught is based on the organization's overall goals. The audience must be taken into consideration in developing the scope and sequence of what is taught.

STRATEGY #5

MINDSET MATTERS
Transform Individual Mindsets and Shift System's Thinking

Whatever the mind can conceive and believe, it will achieve.
—*NAPOLEON HILL*

One of my favorite quotes is by French Philosopher Descartes, "I think, therefore I am." There is much debate as to what Descartes meant by this quote. The way that I conceptualize it is, whatever I am thinking affects my actions (i.e., my choices), which ultimately affect my outcomes. There must be some truth to this as the belief is demonstrated in diverse areas. In various religious texts, there are references to one's thinking and outcomes. In psychology, it is referred to as a self-fulfilling prophecy. In other circles, it is known as the Law of Attraction.

The year after I became Teacher of the Year was very eventful. The career that once brought me so much joy was suddenly causing me to have panic attacks at night, and I never thought in a million years that I would be in that place. Many of you might be in that very place, especially if you have been in education for years. You are just going through the motions on autopilot, you want your students to be successful so you work hard, yet you don't feel the passion anymore for a myriad of reasons, and you wonder if you are good enough, prepared enough, and talented enough to meet the demands of a changing educational landscape. You feel like you are in a rut. I want you to know that you are good enough, and you have the power to either bloom where you are planted or grow on your way.

The Success Principles by Jack Canfield states that a major premise is to take 100% responsibility for your life. In short, we may not be able to control the things that happen to us, but we can control how we react to them. E+R=0. This stands for event + response = outcome. I began to reflect on so many things that happened in my life that I viewed as setbacks. Nevertheless, some things that happened were in my control: my mindset, my attitude, my willingness to grow and learn, and my ability to work with others.

There were also unexpected things that happened professionally as a result of someone else's actions: new curriculum, teacher evaluation system, school leader, and mandates. We now know that whether we chose the event or not, we are 100% in control of how we respond. The power is in our response. How liberating is that? It is in your divine birthright to live and experience the best life and career that you possibly can have. Ultimately, there is not one entity or thing that can keep you from succeeding, except you. We have the choice as both facilitators and participants in learning to see ourselves as creators or victims. If a training session doesn't go as planned, we have another opportunity to recalibrate and do it again.

Principal 2: You have the power!

Nothing can stop you but you.

Author H.T. Hamblin illustrates this best in his book, *Dynamic Thought*. Hamblin says there is nothing that can stop your power but your own doubt and fear. The keynote of success is unbounded confidence. Another word for unbounded confidence is faith. Do you have the confidence to move your professional and personal life forward? One caveat is that our professional practices as educators and our personal lives are inextricably linked. I have seen many successful principals and teachers with their personal lives in shambles as a result of the demands of this job. I am a firm believer that it is our divine birthright to experience success in all areas of our lives. If you dropped dead today or tomorrow, although the impact you made might be lasting, the show will go on. Make sure you take care of yourself and your family, so you can continue to make a difference in the lives of others.

Success Action # 1

Create opportunities for initial success to increase long-term success.

Principal/Teacher-Leader: After teachers see a model lesson or teaching demonstration, have them integrate the strategy and role play with a team to obtain immediate feedback from peers. This creates transparency and a willingness to move beyond isolation. It also helps teachers to overcome their fears of doing something new.

Teacher: Have students build their confidence by recognizing their strengths and building classroom community. Recognize their strengths/giftedness by establishing rituals. At the beginning of each class have students chorally recite a positive affirmation.

Success Action # 2

Be Transparent: Remember Obstacles

Reflect on past obstacles you have overcome and share your triumphs with others.

During my senior year of college, I was twenty-two years old. I was taking nineteen hours in school, completing an internship, and working a part-time job. I had morning sickness throughout the day and could barely muster up the energy to get out of bed, let alone go to school or work. I was depressed, stressed, broke, and broken. I remember being on campus one day, trudging along and seeing one of my professors, Dr. James Ward. Usually, when he would see me he would mispronounce my name or joke about my newest hairdo. However, that day was different. He looked at me with a serious look on his face and said, "Count it all joy, Ms. Carter." He said this at a time when I was at my wit's end and felt like giving up completely. Those six words were like gasoline that filled my empty gas tank. I had been running on fumes and my car was breaking down, and the boost gave me the energy that I needed to keep going.

The week I graduated from college, I was five months pregnant, and I came home to an eviction notice on my door. I looked at the eviction notice and, instead of breaking down, I smiled and remembered to "Count it all joy." Can you imagine how my students felt when I shared this story with them years later? They viewed me as someone relatable, an imperfect person who hadn't made the best decisions, yet still moved forward. I also shared with my students that at eight months pregnant, I started graduate school. I had neither a job nor money, but I persevered. If I could do it, so could they. I started my first teaching assignment when my daughter was six weeks old.

I don't tell this story often, but when I do students often tell me they were on the verge of quitting. The research says that people remember stories more than they remember "facts." Of course, the story should relate to the concept that you are teaching or presenting. Stories are about creating connections, for when we connect with others psychologically we are more open to learning. Self-disclosure is scary because we put ourselves in a vulnerable position. I may not be the "best" teacher or presenter, but I know that I have value and bring value to the classroom. This is evidenced by my self-awareness and self-concept, by my personal and professional accomplishments including being recognized as "Teacher of the Year," and by being one of the top employees within my college.

Fear and limiting beliefs about ourselves and others limit harnessing the potential of our people and programs. As a former literacy coach, I once encountered a teacher who told me that she couldn't implement a strategy I taught her because the students just couldn't do it. I asked her if she would try any way and she did. A few weeks later, she told me that she had seen so much improvement in her class. I replied, "But you said the students couldn't do it." Ms. Johnson informed me that she really felt like she couldn't do it, and that it was easier to blame the students. That remark made me pause to do some deep introspection. Some of us are so afraid of failing that we won't even try, much like some students. Failure is an integral part of success. If we are to transform our classrooms, we must create space for true growth and the space for innovation in which one is willing to take a risk. This flies in the face of mantras such as "Failure is not an option." It should be. Honest conversations about grit and perseverance along with a growth mindset deal with experiencing some tension or being uncomfortable yet still moving forward.

Success Action # 3: Improve Verbal Communication
Use verbal communication constructively.

Words are powerful, and we have the ability to construct or destruct based on what we say. I have realized that often when we continue to focus on lack, we begin to experience more lack. So I have learned to affirm or speak what I expect. Even when things are not appearing as I want them to appear at the moment.

I have encountered educators and students from all walks of life. Imagine if we were intentional about the words we use when speaking to each other. Are our words giving life, or do they suck the life from others? When engaging in self-talk, do you affirm or denigrate yourself? If you think and continue to speak that things are the worse they have ever been, that will forever be your reality. Are you a victim or are you a creator? Once you recognize that you are not powerless, you will achieve greatness beyond your wildest dreams, and you will consequently inspire others around you to achieve greatness beyond their wildest dreams.

Wood (2013) asserts that engaging in dual perspective is a critical guideline for effective verbal communication. It is important to be mindful of the words we speak and be person-centered and aware of other perspectives. Dual perspective is not abandoning your perspective, but it is honoring others' points of view and your own. It is also using language appropriately.

Success Action # 4
Share stories that are relatable.

Let's take a look at some notable people who overcame adversity:
Albert Einstein
Napoleon Hill
Maya Angelou
Oprah Winfrey

In order to develop a master-mindset and help others develop one, help them to understand the power of effective communication.

Self-Fulfilling Prophecy

A self-fulfilling prophecy occurs when a person's expectation of an event, and her or his subsequent behavior based on those expectations, makes the outcome more likely to occur than would otherwise be true (Watzlawick, 2005). A self-fulfilling prophecy involves four stages:

1. Holding an expectation (for you or for others).
2. Behaving in accordance with that expectation.
3. Bringing the expectation to pass.
4. Reinforcing the original expectation.

Another way to look at this is through the Pygmalion effect. Research shows that teacher expectations influence student performance (Rosenthal and Jacobsen, 1968). Positive expectations may influence students positively and negative expectations may influence them negatively. When designing professional learning for teachers, one must do so from a strengths-based perspective versus a deficit-based one. As school leaders, we must be careful to not create a brushstroke that labels and thus marginalizes teachers as lazy, unmotivated, and uncaring just as we must be careful about not doing that with students. **"When we expect certain behaviors of others, we are likely to act in ways that make the expected behavior more likely to occur"** (Rosenthal and Babad, 1985). Oftentimes, these expectations come true based on the actions we take. If you lack trust in me, it is natural that I will lack trust in you. You must be the type of leader you would want to follow.

Success Strategy # 5: Affirm Yourself
Create or say affirmations that reflect your positive expectations.

Personal Affirmations

I prosper at every turn. I deserve prosperity. I am worthy of living the life of my dreams.

The more grateful I am, the more reasons I find to be grateful. I pay my bills with love as I know abundance flows freely through me. I reframe thinking that causes me to continue to experience lack. My well overflows, easy come, easy flow. I am living life abundantly. I have all that I need and want.

Affirmations at Work

I recognize the unique talents and giftedness in myself, my students, and my colleagues.

I am solution-oriented.

I expect the best so I give my best.

I am an awesome teacher who faces fears, embraces change, and continuously learns.

I am a transformational leader who inspires people, promotes positive changes, and achieves sustained results.

I am a fierce facilitator of learning and this professional learning session achieves its intended outcomes.

I am excited that resources are available to support our educational objectives and goals.

I am harnessing my potential and leveraging the giftedness, knowledge, and skills of others.

The Power of Perception

> CHANGE THE WAY YOU LOOK AT THINGS AND
> THE THINGS YOU LOOK AT CHANGE.
> —WAYNE W. DYER

Imagine obtaining the job in education you really wanted. You are fired up and ready to learn all you can. You are ready to take the bull by the horns and not only meet expectations, but exceed them. The Sunday night before your job begins, you lay your clothes out, prepare your lunch, and anticipate the possibilities. Will your co-workers accept you? Will you like them? The questions seem endless.

You toss and turn all night, and the alarm goes off. You barely slept. You are grateful that you've made it. All of the education gotten, experience garnered, and trainings attended have prepared you for this moment. You have arrived. You confidently approach the doors to your brand new assignment, open them, and look around. *Great things are going to happen here,* you think to yourself. Fast forward a month into the job, your spirits are pretty high, you're working hard, you are seeing some progress, and the honeymoon phase is slowly starting to fade away.

Perception refers to how we see things. We have a tremendous amount of power in how we choose to see an event and how we respond to it. For example, if you failed a major exam, which prevents you from getting into a program, you could choose to give up or forge ahead exploring alternative options. Maybe I need to study harder or study differently. Perhaps, I thought I was suited for this, but I am really more suited for something else. How we conceptualize events affects our response to them. How we perceive others affects the way we communicate.

When you understand the law of compensation, you will realize that your whole life is centered on the spirit of giving—giving love, appreciation, praise, time, support, efforts, and substance. The "comeback" will always follow.

And don't just do your share: go the extra mile. It is not enough to give love and friendship; give it back with an extra measure. Likewise, with justice, kindness, cooperation, and devotion, give back dividends.

In any situation, find some way to give. Give your way into a new consciousness. This is one of the most important starting points in the study of Truth, and the law of compensation is one of Truth's most fundamental laws.

How powerful is this? It is in thinking that we find the key to this law. If there is something we don't like, we must change our mental attitudes and how we "see" the event.

Perception and Thinking

> *It has become something of a cliché to observe that if we do not love ourselves, we cannot love anyone else. This is true enough, but it is only part of the picture. If we do not love ourselves, it is almost impossible to believe fully that we are loved by someone else. It is almost impossible to accept love. It is almost impossible to receive love. No matter what our partner does to show that he or she cares, we do not experience the devotion as convincing because we do not feel lovable to ourselves.*
> —Nathaniel Branden (The Psychology of Romantic Love)

Our thinking impacts perceptions, and inaccurate perceptions about ourselves and others can lead to a host of unwanted outcomes. If I don't think of myself as worthy of romantic love if I were to receive it, I wouldn't know how to handle it. If I have a poor self-esteem, it may lead to my having a negative perception of events or remaining stuck in a situation I need to get away from because I view myself as powerless. Harriet Tubman was a slave just like millions of other black people during that time period. Yet, her perception about the future, coupled with her dogged determination and thinking, allowed her to conceptualize that there had to have been more. Her thinking served as a catalyst for her action. Have you ever wondered how two people with similar circumstances end up with two very different outcomes? I can almost guarantee that their mindsets and perceptions of circumstances and resources played a role. If there are two teachers in the same school with similar sets of students, one teacher has a tremendous success and the other does not. The same can be said about two people from the same neighborhood with similar types of backgrounds: one becomes college educated; the other one goes to jail. Yes, there may be other variables, but more often than not, our outcomes are related to choices. Our choices are related to our thinking as to what we think is possible and what we think isn't.

Perception Matters

A Different Look at Failure

In Napoleon Hill's *Think and Grow Rich,* there is a story that really puts this into perspective. Hill (1966) tells the story of an uncle of R.U. Darby. During the gold rush days, he was hit with "gold rush fever." He started by using a pick and shovel. He discovered a shiny ore, but needed more equipment. He excitedly went and told others who also caught the fever and pulled their resources to buy some heavy machinery. They experienced initial success, but then the results began to taper off and they drilled on and on. They finally decided to quit. They sold the machinery to a "junk" man for a few hundred dollars. Some "junk" men are not dumb, as some thought. This particular junk man was quite shrewd and called a mining engineer to look at the mine and do a little calculating. The engineer advised that the project had failed because the owner was not familiar with the fault lines. His calculations showed that the vein could be found just three feet below the surface where Darby stopped drilling. Guess what—that is exactly where it was found. The junk man took millions of dollars in ore from the mine because he knew to seek expert counsel before giving up.

Hill reminds us that there are many lessons in this story.

1. We often give up before experiencing the breakthrough or achieving our goals.
2. If we don't know how to do something, we can seek the expertise of others who are successful in the same endeavor. We can take classes, we can read books, and we can search on the internet. Have you ever looked something up on YouTube to learn how to do it? Have you ever had to go to the doctor for a diagnosis to get to the root cause of a medical issue in order to alleviate it?
3. We make assumptions about people based on labels and our own frames of reference (i.e., "junk man"). We do this to others based

on our belief systems and frames of reference, which influence our perceptions. We like to put people into boxes based on race, ethnicity, religious affiliation, sexual orientation, social status, etc.

4. The way we label people or situations can lead to confirmation bias. Confirmation bias is the tendency to seek information that supports our values and beliefs while discounting or ignoring information that doesn't (Floyd, 2011).

STRATEGY #6

LEADERS ARE VISIONARY

Vision is the art of seeing what is invisible to others.
—*JONATHAN SWIFT*

I n *The Game of Life* by Florence Shinn, Shinn expresses the correlation between thinking and vision. Shinn (1925) says that "The Master Thinker is an artist and is careful to paint only divine designs upon the canvas of his mind." He or she paints these pictures with masterly strokes of power and decision, having perfect confidence that there is no power to mar perfection and that they shall manifest in his or her life; the ideal made real.

What do you envision for your future? Where do you see yourself one year from now, five years from now, and ten years from now? Research indicates that the most meaningful learning happens when students are engaged in authentic activities that ask them to think and behave like chemists, computer programmers, mathematicians, engineers or archeologists — that is, when they are engaged in activities that mirror the real-life tasks of professionals (Tate, 2012). In essence, students are more engaged when they are able to see themselves in these particular roles. These roles are potentially mirroring their future. As a result of exposure, they are able to see something they may not have even thought about before.

Visualization Defined

So what is visualization? Visualization is the process of creating a mental image or intention of what you want to happen or feel (Quinn, 2013). Research shows that many athletes use this technique in order to achieve their goals. Sports psychologists also recognize visualization. If everything you needed for success was already available to you, how would that change things for you? Your future success is determined by your present actions. Reaching your performance goal requires partnering with the right resources. It is not a passive activity.

Peak performance is a decision. Envision winning. Believe it is possible. Be ready to do anything to make it happen. Conviction in your abilities is powerful. Here is the bottom line: believing something is possible increases your odds of success.

Your mind is unable to discriminate between imagination and reality. This is why your dreams appear so real. Harness the power of your imagination and visualize your success. Sports psychologists talk about visualization a lot. It is THE most popular mindset tool used by athletes. It needs to be used correctly to be most effective.

STRATEGY #7

TAKE ACTION

Now that you have set your goals, how will you implement them? An essential element of organizational success is learning. After you identify the organizational goals, how do you know which learning intervention to select? Learning is not always implementing a professional development workshop. In terms of resources, "Almost every non-training tool is faster and cheaper to implement than instruction. That is why instruction, should be like surgery, a last resort." Many organizations invest thousands of dollars into training when other forms of learning can be implemented. The training ends up being a waste of time and money if it is not monitored, adjusted, and sustained. These things have to be taken into consideration when choosing an intervention.

According to Guila Muir, author of *Instructional Design That Soars: Shaping What You Know into Classes That Inspire*, there are three questions one must consider in designing instruction:

1. What is the problem?
2. Is group training the only solution?
3. How and when do you know if the problem has been solved?

In order to create buy-in and to really have multiple perspectives, it is important that participants receiving the intervention be asked the essential three questions. As an organization, the decision can be made regarding what type of learning intervention is effective. Some may choose to move forward with training and others may choose to implement another type of learning intervention. Avoid the urge to provide a training session because it is a great idea.

What problem are you trying to solve? What goal are you trying to achieve?

Here are some examples:

Who: Superintendent, mid-size district.
Problem: There is a high turnover rate of teachers at under-resourced schools.

Who: Principal, highly resourced school.
Problem: Gifted students are not growing academically.

Who: Deputy Superintendent, rural school district.
Problem: Writing scores have decreased in the secondary schools.

Who: Asst. Principal, urban school.
Problem: There is a school-wide increase in discipline referrals among certain demographics.

You can identify the problem using surveys, interviews, and other available data (Muir, 2013). As you begin to explore the issue, you may be able to explore further to clearly define the issue before moving to the next step.

STRATEGY #8

EXPLORE NON-TRAINING SOLUTIONS

Do we have to meet again?

More options for solving issues with less time and money.

Is group training or a meeting the only solution?

Save time!

Save money!

Leverage resources!

Use easier, cheaper, more effective solutions to solve the issue? The problem may not necessarily be a training problem but one that is related to communication, leadership, interpersonal relationships, systems, and organizational culture. These are some learning alternatives that you might consider before creating a professional development session.

1. Provide feedback via coaching.
2. Providing better resources, tools, or equipment.
3. Creating a job aid, eBook, or template. If there is an issue with lesson plans, provide an example of a lesson plan that meets the criteria of the expectation. If there is an issue with school improvement plans, provide an example of one that meets the expectation.

4. Send a memo.
5. Use teleconferencing or virtual meetings.
6. Use social media and disseminate a quickie how-to via Facebook, Twitter, or some other medium.
7. Facilitate a brainstorming/planning session.
8. Document procedures of best practices to promote sustainability.
9. Develop interventions for non-compliant stakeholders.
10. Develop checklists.
11. Introduce incentives.
12. Create a newsletter.
13. Initiate organizational change with focus groups and interviews.
14. Provide a lesson demonstration with follow-up and feedback using:
    a. Observation/feedback
    b. I do (expert)
    c. We do (collaboration)
    d. You do (demonstration)
    e. Progress monitoring/evaluation/celebration
15. Provide videos or screencasts.
16. Celebrate wins.
17. Provide an online learning hub.
18. Promote innovation.
19. Use reflective journals.
20. Learning walks.
21. Participate in feedback circles.

Explore all alternatives to training first. There are multiple ways to promote changes in knowledge, attitudes, and skills. Training should be the intervention of last resort (Muir, 2013).

How will you know an intervention was successful and a problem was solved? What would be different?

Leaders have vision. When leaders discuss the problems they are able to "see" in advance what will change when the problem is solved. This helps one to decide if one needs to implement ACHIEVE, which is Content,

Organization, Delivery, and Evaluation in creating a training session. People in the previous examples visualized their situations in the following ways:

Who: Superintendent, mid-size district.
Problem: There is a high turnover rate of teachers at under-resourced schools.

Solution (What will have changed?): There is a decreased turnover rate as a result of increased resources, sustained leadership, and additional support, which has led to retention of high-yield teachers in schools that need them most.

Who: Principal, highly resourced school.
Problem: Gifted students are not growing academically.
Solution (What will have changed?): There is increased student achievement among gifted students.

Who: Deputy Superintendent, rural school district.
Problem: Writing scores have decreased in the secondary schools.
Solution: Writing scores have increased by 10 percentage points among secondary students.

Who: Asst. Principal, urban school.
Problem: There is a school-wide increase in discipline referrals among certain demographics.
Solution: By the end of the year, there was a 25% decrease in discipline referrals among African-American girls.

Case Study
Who: Principal
Problem: There were too many meetings and very limited progress.
Solution: There was a decrease in meetings by 20% and an increase in the use of digital communication with progress monitoring checks and balances on initiatives implemented.

Let's take an in-depth look.

A new principal held numerous meetings at the beginning of the school year. Teachers and other employees began to dread the meetings because they were perceived as boring, pointless, and monotonous. Teachers wanted to spend more time planning and actually completing their tasks versus talking about the work. The principal began to hear the rumblings and wanted to do something that created buy-in, maximized professional learning, increased engagement, and implementation of strategies that led to more gains.

The principal sent out surveys and solicited feedback regarding the meetings. She also created a focus group with various stakeholders to garner additional perspective. The findings were clear. The meetings were unproductive and entirely too long. Some who were responsible for facilitating were perceived as monotone presenters who either lacked skills in communicating or facilitating. The principal formed a special committee to review ways to revamp meetings and provide additional opportunities for professional learning that was engaging, relevant, and meaningful. The committee read a few articles, books, and they extracted best practices. One major suggestion was to establish norms at the beginning of each meeting. Shortly thereafter, most staff used norms in various meetings held in and around campus. Additionally, committee members paid attention to feedback regarding meetings that were perceived as successfully presented and facilitated by one of the teacher-leaders. The principal asked her to develop an "Effective Meeting Tips and Tools Checklist." Soon all members of the leadership team and department chairs were using the checklist. Meetings improved considerably, and most lasted less than an hour. In addition, other interventions were considered such as memos and short videos with progress monitoring and accountability instead of meetings. This situation did not require a professional development workshop or program. The principal used a "study group" or committee to identify an easy solution (the use of norms), and it then used the subject-matter expertise of one employee to create a checklist and the expertise of a computer teacher to create a two-minute screen cast to show how to create short videos and screencasts. The principal shared the "Effective Meeting Tips and Tools" checklist with other principals and soon principals across the district were employing similar practices. In a survey completed a few months later, the principal found that although there were fewer meetings, they were more productive, and that other forms of professional learning were used and maximized around the campus.

There are a variety of ways that learning can occur on a campus.

STRATEGY #9

FOSTER BRAIN-BASED LEARNING

Learning is an active process. We learn by doing.
Only knowledge that is used sticks in your mind.
—DALE CARNEGIE

Concept Map for This Section

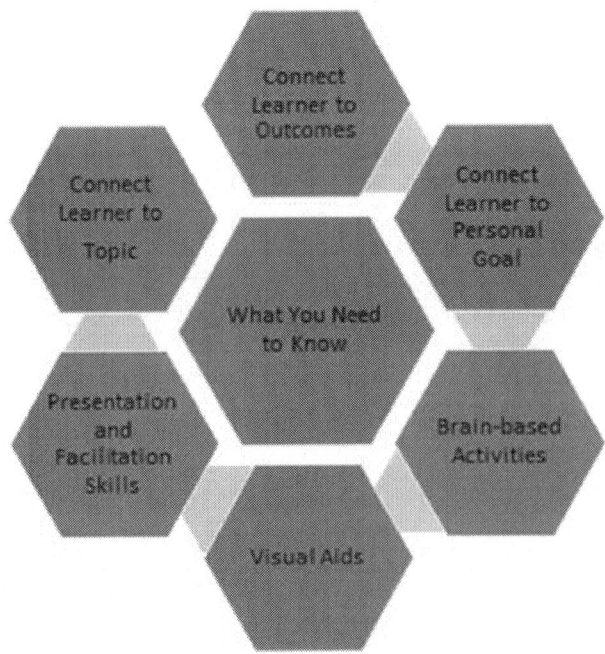

How Adults Learn

Just as it is important to engage children, those who present and facilitate adult learning should be engaging as well. This information is important to those leading a professional learning session whether they are teachers, counselors, or administrators. Best practices in andragogy or adult learning theory should be included in professional development. Adults learn best when meeting the following criteria:

1. They are *actively engaged* participants in the learning.

When people are present but not engaged, active learning is not occurring. The most important part is in the doing. This is where the learning occurs. Whether conducting a face-to-face presentation or a virtual class, make it active and participatory.

Strategies

a. Reflection/journaling
b. Partner share
c. Discussion
d. Role play
e. Graphic organizers
f. Jigsaw
g. Drawing
h. Brainstorming
i. Music
j. Inquiry
k. Opportunities to teach/subject-matter expertise
l. Informal learning
m. Social media
n. Technology
o. Peer coaching
p. Mnemonics
q. Affirmation
r. Celebrations
s. Feedback

2. *Connect* with participants' experiences and emotions.

The learning experience is maximized when it hooks into something you want participants to learn or do.

Past: Connecting with a participant's former experiences makes the learning relevant.

Present: Focusing on participants' immediate needs. They will learn better if the content helps them to become better in some way and increase their knowledge and skills.

Future: Focus on participants' future goals. Help participants monitor progress and have a sense of accomplishment.

3. Acknowledge wins.

When student mastery occurs, or when an individual goal is achieved, how will you celebrate? Celebrations are important because they engender motivation for increased success.

4. Demonstrate that you care about the participants.

Essential questions
    Desired learning/outcomes
    What knowledge, skills, and abilities do you want participants to have as a result of attending your session?

Actions

Review

Evaluate

STRATEGY #10

PRESENTATION SKILLS MATTER

Have you ever heard someone present who kept you humored, riveted, engaged, and captivated? As a result, the time just seemed to fly by? Conversely, have you ever heard someone who was credentialed, yet very monotone and inaudible? You struggled to pay attention and focus because you knew what they were saying was important. You jotted down a few notes, but when it was over, you felt like it was a complete waste of time. The speaker just read from the PowerPoint slides, line by line, with his or her back facing the audience. You felt like a prisoner, and this "important" meeting was a snore presentation. You would've been better off reading a book. Finally, it is over and you are able to escape.

When you are training, you will have various roles. You might serve as presenter, facilitator, and coach all at the same training session. With that in mind, it is important to remember that just because you told them, doesn't mean you taught it, and yes, presentations skills matter.

Presentation skills consist of both verbal and nonverbal communication. Here is a quick checklist to keep in mind:

1. Are you making eye contact with the audience or are you just facing the slides and reading aloud the whole time?
2. Do you have voice inflection and energy or are you speaking in a monotone?
3. How is your rate of speech? Are you speaking at a moderate pace, or is it too fast or too slow?
4. How is your pausing? Do you pause for effect? Are there too many pauses?
5. Do you involve the audience while you are presenting or is it all about the sage on the stage?
6. Do you stand in just one place? Are you movements intentional or distracting?
7. Do you appear to be poised and confident or is your nervousness visible and distracting?
8. Do you adjust your presentation based on the verbal and nonverbal feedback from the audience?
9. Do you intersperse a balance of emotional appeal, ethical appeal, and logical appeal or do you just use facts and figures?
10. Do you use stories to help the audience make connections with the data?
11. Do you present in a logical, sequential matter, or do you sound like you are all over the place?
12. How do you gauge if you are effective?

This may seem like a lot, but remember how you felt when you were imprisoned during someone else's presentation. Well, we certainly don't want anyone to feel that way during your presentation.

Presenting while teaching or training means helping you give information, so that they can get it.

How can you present with the brain in mind?

In *Sizzle and Substance* by Eric Jensen, Jensen (1998) provides some helpful strategies:

1) Limit the content.

Oftentimes, we try to cover too much information and end up presenting way more information than we should, which ends up resulting in brain overload.

2) Humanize your content.

Make the information relevant and meaningful to the learners. Don't focus on content at the expense of the people.

3) Customize your presentation.

Every audience is unique. Treat each training opportunity as new, even if you are presenting the same information. Research the audience demographics to make sure that you are able to make it meaningful and valuable for them. People are more apt to apply information that they deem is valuable.

4) Over-prepare.

Review your information to make sure that it is accurate and relevant. Make sure that you are knowledgeable of the content in order to effectively teach it or train over it.

5. Have a strong opening.

Primacy is based on the first impression the audience forms. If you fail to get their attention at the very beginning, it is going to be hard to keep it for the rest of the presentation.

6. Avoid jargon.

Use terms that people can relate to. Too much jargon may turn off an audience. Use metaphors, examples, and analogies to make complex information simple.

7. Develop a rapport.

Show audience members that you are interested in them. Use gestures, examples, and humor. Get them involved by asking questions and involving them through the presentation. Involving the audience will enhance their perception of you and their memory.

Tips and Techniques for Avoiding Bore and Snore Presentations

1. Use novelty items such as models, toys, balls, or balloons that increase interest and engagement.
2. Have visual elements to increase clarity and understanding. You can also ask learners to construct visual images to help increase their understanding of course material.
3. Tell a story with emotional appeal to generate more interest.
4. Identify the experts in the room, ask them to be a part of a panel, and interview them in front of the audience.
5. Allow learners to participate in teach backs. They find a partner and summarize what was said, reviewing a particular section to reinforce concepts.

VISUAL AIDS ARE VITAL

The Environment

The learning environment is very important when teaching. A theme is a unique way to add value and promote value and learning. Conversely, a theme can also come off as gimmicky and futile if not implemented correctly. Themes will positively impact the environment when they fit the occasion and are related to the subject matter. Meir (2000) states that a theme can aid the learning process when it does the following:

- Helps tie the subject matter together.
- Creates a fun and engaging environment.
- Relaxes and energizes the learner.
- Inspires creativity.
- Humanizes the learning process.
- Promotes brainstorming and collaboration.
- Provides visual aids for the environment.

Types of Themes

Journey	Events/Sports	Other Ideas
Cruise	Olympics	Movies
Bus ride	Nascar	Music
Plane ride	Final four	Amusement park
Mountain climbing	Super bowl	Carnival
Camping	World series	Luau

Hiking	Baseball	Jungle
Space	Football	A day at the beach
	Basketball	Gardening
	Soccer	Literature

Holidays/Seasons

Spring
Summer
Fall
Winter

See It and Believe It: Making Visuals Work

Visual images are used to communicate important information. From pictures to symbols, visual aids have been used throughout history to convey information. When you think of the color red, what comes to mind? When you think of the color green, what comes to mind? Words and images can accelerate the learning process.

Presentation Aids

Pictures can be used in study guides and to increase interest in lectures. Videos, Power Point, Prezi, Emaze, Animoto, and Canva are great tools that can make presentations visually appealing and engaging.

Brainstorming

Using charts to help visualize goals for short- and long-term planning can be very effective. Pictures can be used in various ways:

- Creating graphic organizers to visualize info
- Mind mapping
- Seeing things chronologically
- Action planning
- Evaluation methods

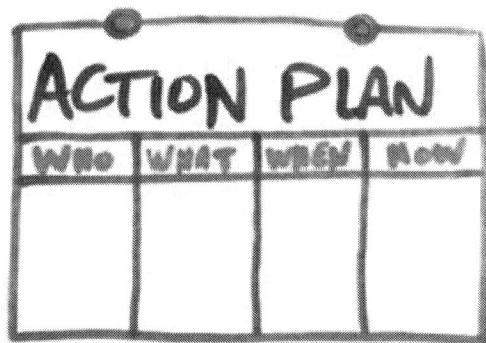

Meetings

Meetings can be enhanced with the following:

- Handouts
- Checklists
- Emails
- Presentations
- Decision-making aids
- Meeting facilitation
- Manuals
- Reports

Knowledge Assessment

Graphic organizers and shell pictograms are useful when participants fill in the blanks with words and pictures. This can be used as a check for understanding activity. The participants can work in pairs or alone.

Timely Tips for Visual Aids

1. Limit your text to no more than three lines per slide.
2. Include a visual image on each slide.
3. If your PowerPoint can stand alone, it is too wordy. If it is designed to be shared with other notes, they can be included in the notes section.
4. There should be contrast between the font color and background. A dark font should have a light background, but a light font should have a dark background.
4. Use a font that is not difficult to read.
5. Make sure there are not any grammatical errors. If you can have someone take a look at it before you present, that may be helpful. Errors take away from your credibility.
6. Show short clips from movies or television shows to illustrate a point.
7. Include images on your handouts to increase interest, clarity, and interactivity.
8. Use posters, humor, and items throughout the training to visually reinforce important concepts.

STRATEGY #12

CULTIVATE INFORMAL LEARNING

In his book, *Informal Learning: Rediscovering the Natural Pathways That Inspire Innovation and Performance,* Jay Cross likens the difference between formal and informal training to riding on a bus versus a bike:

- With the formal learning bus, "the driver decides where the bus is going; the passengers are along for the ride."
- When on the informal learning bike, "the rider chooses the destination, the speed, and the route."

Self-directed learning is an integral component in adult learning theory. How many of you have learned something by reading a blog or Facebook post? Perhaps you attended a conference and the biggest takeaway didn't come from a session but an informal conversation you had in the hallway. It is important to acknowledge expertise gleaned from these types of situations. Leaders are not just concerned with the learning, because they desire application and a change in practice. Informal does not mean unintentional. Informal learning is a huge strategy for obtaining results as schools can use it to do the following:

- Improve job-embedded knowledge, efficiency, and productivity.
- Generate fresh ideas and increase innovation.
- Problem solve issues concerning problems of practice.
- Reduce stress and improve absenteeism by fostering a collegial and collaborative environment.
- Invest in resources that will yield the most return.
- Cut costs and improve responsiveness with self-service learning.

These opportunities can be fostered via social learning networks such as Facebook, Linkedin, Instagram, and SnapChat. They also can be fostered through building a sense of community and fostering teamwork as a part of the school's culture.

Informal learning is powerful, but it's not new. As long as people have learned how to perform work-related tasks by observing and interacting with others, **informal learning** has played a significant role in training and development (Carliner, 2014).

Informal Learning Check-In

How do you evaluate informal learning within your organization?

- How do workers learn informally?

- What did workers learn informally?

- How can workers receive recognition for their informal learning?

- What is the extent of participation in various informal learning activities?

- What is the extent of satisfaction with various resources used for informal learning?

- In what ways does the organization benefit from informal learning by workers?

- Which informal learning efforts that the organization formally supports are providing tangible benefits to the organization?

- How can our organization(s) better support informal learning efforts?

STRATEGY #13

Promote a Culture of Continuous Improvement

Collaborative learning is an important element in leveraging leadership for learning (Carter Sackey, 2015). *PLCs, learning communities, communities of practice, professional learning teams,* and *critical friends groups* are all terms used to describe individual and collective professional learning of educators in schools (Avila, 2009). Hord (1997) found that PLCs may be challenging to define because they are not programs or prescriptions but structures embedded within the school that lead to cycles of continuous improvement. Therefore, there are various definitions to describe PLCs (Jones et al., 2013). Protheroe (2008) described PLCs as a concept that schools use to leverage collective intelligence and expand educator capabilities to increase student achievement. Hord defined *professional learning communities* as educators working collaboratively to improve their practice and increase student outcomes on an ongoing basis. Another conceptualization of PLCs is collective inquiry and action research by educators on an ongoing basis to better serve students (DuFour, 2006). A synthesis of these descriptions illustrates that the goal of PLCs is for educators to engage in learning on a continuous basis to build individual and collective capacity in order to increase student success.

Research has shown there is an academic achievement gap based on race and socioeconomics (Killion & Roy, 2009). Consequently, improving student achievement among subpopulations is a significant concern in schools across the country. Public schools have an unprecedented mandate to ensure all students learn at high levels (DuFour, 2004; Mizell et al., 2011). A comprehensive review of the literature revealed that high-performing schools with high percentages of minority and socioeconomically disadvantaged students have a collaborative culture, transparent practice, and focus on results (Bitterman, 2010; Conzemius & Morganti-Fisher, 2012; Hord, 2004; Mizell et al., 2011). The issue is there are still many schools in which teachers work in isolation (Easton, 2011). These schools often follow a model of a teacher-centered versus a learner-centered approach, and quality job-embedded professional learning may not be occurring (Hord, 2004). Notably, PLCs may not be the only environment in which all students are consistently achieving; however, the research indicates PLCs can make a significant impact (Hord, 2004). A key focus of the PLC is job-embedded learning (Hirsh & Hord, 2012; Killion & Roy, 2009). As a result, the leverage point for refining and strengthening the day-to-day performance and practice of educators is to increase the effectiveness of professional learning (Hirsh & Hord, 2012).

Professional Development for School Improvement

Successful professional development is a blend of experiences that "empowers (a) individual educators, (b) educational teams, and (c) the educational organization to improve (d) curriculum, (e) instruction, and (f) student assessment in order to (g) facilitate student growth and development" (Gordon, 2004, p. 5). School improvement is necessary for an increase in student outcomes. Not all change leads to school improvement; however, school improvement does not take place without change (Gordon, 2004). An essential element in PLCs is learning. Significant learning is learning that results in lasting change (Fink & Fink, 2009).

The PLC process provides the conduit for powerful professional development that builds staff capacity (DuFour, 2014). Capacity building through continuous job-embedded professional learning leads to successful schools (Gordon, 2004). DuFour (2014) found that student learning improves as a result of an ongoing focus on improved adult learning. DuFour illustrated various districts in which student achievement had significantly increased. An example was District 54 in Illinois, a majority–minority district. In 2005–2006, the district set a stretch goal in which 90% of its students would be able to demonstrate mastery in the language arts and math state assessments. Only 75% of students' demonstrated mastery and none of the schools met the 90/90 target. Within five years, however, 19 of the 27 schools were at benchmark, and the district reported it is because of the implementation and sustainability of the PLC process as a school improvement vehicle (DuFour, 2014). PLCs can be either very effective or ineffective depending on how they are implemented (Easton, 2011). Consequently, these results illustrate the need for standards of professional learning.

Standards for Professional Development/Learning

Standards and their importance continue to be at the forefront of many educational discussions (Fisher & Frey, 2013; Hirsh & Hord, 2012; Hirsh & Killion, 2007). For educators, Learning Forward, with the contribution of 40 professional associations and education organizations, developed the *Standards for Professional Learning*, the third iteration of standards that outline the essential components of professional development that lead to improved student outcomes, supportive leadership, and effective teaching practice (Hirsh & Hord, 2012; "Standards," n.d.).

The term *professional development* has evolved to *professional learning* as it focuses on teachers being an active part of the learning process and emphasizes learning and the continuous cycle of inquiry and improvement (Hirsh & Hord, 2012; Hirsh & Killion, 2007). These standards embody an andragogical construct and enroll educators as active partners in learning to determine the content and context for the learning based on student data and to take leadership roles to facilitate and advocate effective professional learning (Hirsh & Hord, 2012).

Implementation of PLCs has demonstrated promise for sustainable school improvement (Peppers, 2014). An effective implementation must focus on the learning of the adults responsible for teaching and learning (Easton, 2011). How can these standards and the evolution of professional development lead to growing the talent within your organizations and optimizing student achievement? When adults are involved in ongoing, job-embedded learning, significant change occurs.

STRATEGY #14

EVALUATE THE PROCESS

How to Measure Training Results

Evaluation and measurement are valuable tools to internalizing a results-based culture and tracking progress. Phillips and Stone (2002) find that when looking for evidence of accountability in training, one of the key issues is what data should you review and what you should look for. The Kilpatrick Model is a well-known model that was developed in 1959, updated in 1975, and again in 1994. The model was later expanded in 2000 with one additional level added to the initial four by Phillips and Stone (2002). This model is in line with Learning Forward's focus of job-embedded learning.

Evaluation Framework

LEVEL AND TYPE OF DATA	FOCUS OF THE DATA	SUMMARY OF HOW THE DATA IS USEFUL
Level 1: Reaction and/or satisfaction and planned action.	Focus is on the training program, the facilitator, and how application might occur.	Reaction data reveals what the target population thinks of the program. How satisfied they are with the program. Planned actions/implementation as a result of the program. Planned actions/implementation can be used as a focal point for follow-up evaluation which may lead to program improvements.
Level 2: Learning	Focus is on the participant and various support mechanisms for learning.	Learning is focused on measuring the extent to which the desired attitudes, principles, knowledge, facts, processes, procedures,

		techniques, or skills have been learned by participants. It is more difficult to measure learning than to merely solicit a reaction. Measures should be objective and quantifiable of how requirements are understood and applied. This data is used to confirm that participant learning has occurred as a result of the initiative. This data is also used to make adjustments in the program content, design, and delivery.
Level 3: Behavior Job Application/and or implementation.	Focus is on the participant, the work setting, and support mechanisms for applying learning.	This measures behavioral change and specific application of knowledge and skills. This is knowing versus doing. This is measured after the training has been implemented in the work setting. It should address what is and what is not working.
Level 4: Impact	Focus is on the impact of the training process on specific organizational outcomes.	This determines the training's influence in improving organizational performance. Objective data such as cost savings, output increases, time savings, or quality

		improvements.
		Subjective data such as increases in employee satisfaction, increase in teacher and student and/or teacher retention, and decrease in absenteeism, etc., would also be taken into consideration.
		Generating organizational impact would include collecting data before and after the training and linking the outcomes of the training to the appropriate business measures by analyzing results for improvement (or lack thereof).
Level 5: Return on Investment (ROI)	Focus is on the monetary benefits as a result of the training.	This is an evaluation of the monetary value of the business impact of training. The business impact is that data is converted to a monetary value in order to apply it to the formula to calculate a ROI. This shows the true value of the program in terms of the organization's objectives. It is presented as an ROI value or cost benefit ratio, usually expressed as a percentage. An improvement in a business impact measure as a result of training may not necessarily produce a positive ROI (e.g., if the training is expensive).

		In *Determining Return of Investment for Professional Development in Education,* Kosloski and Reed (2009) provide an excellent example of the different levels of the Kilpatrick Model and evaluating ROI. A quick Google search should yield the study.
Intangible Benefits	Focus is on the added value of the training in non-monetary terms.	Intangible data is data that either cannot or should not be converted to monetary value. This has nothing to do with the importance of the data; it addresses the lack of objectivity of the data and the inability to convert the data to monetary values. Sometimes it may be too expensive to convert certain data to monetary data. Other times management and other stakeholders are satisfied with intangible data. For example, a training program may result in increased student achievement but it may be a challenge to measure ROI as schools are significantly different than traditional businesses.

Chart is adapted from *How to Measure Training Results*
by Jack J. Phillips and Ron Drew Stone.

Kilpatrick's Model is a well-known model in learning and development. A quick synopsis of this model is the following:

1. Learners' feelings about what they learned
2. Knowledge attained
3. Improved performance
4. Return on staff development investment

There are countless web articles and various selections of his books available for more in-depth study.

Other ways to evaluate learning is to develop creative ways for people to assess their own changes in knowledge, attitudes, or skills. You can use pre- and post-tests, the dot method, discussions about whether participants compare what they know now versus what they knew before, and implementation of learner-created action-plans with built-in progress monitoring.

STRATEGY #15

CREATE FEEDBACK LOOPS

Feedback is vitally important to learning. Feedback is information the learners receive to assess their progress. Feedback should come from the instructor or the organizational environment. Feedback should be either confirming (to let the learner know that that he or she has attained the partial or complete objective) or corrective (to let the learner alter responses).

Here is what the research tells us:

- Frequent, timely, specific feedback helps to improve performance.
- Feedback the learner perceives as directed toward the task helps to improve performance.
- Feedback that the learner perceives as criticism could hinder or reduce performance contingent upon how the critique is provided.
- Delayed feedback could be more effective on what learners perceive as complex tasks (feedback given too soon can confuse the learner with information overload).

Confirming versus Disconfirming Communication

Managing Difficult Conversations

Harvard Negotiation Project researchers define difficult conversations as the following:

Anytime we feel vulnerable, we care deeply about what is being said or discussed and with whom we are discussing it, the issue at hand is important and the outcome is uncertain, and there is potential for us to experience the conversation as difficult (Cardon, 2016).

Handling Difficult Conversations

1. View the conflict as an opportunity.

The exchange of perspectives and competing ideas reflect open and honest communication. If there is no conflict, employees are not likely to be voicing their true perspectives. Conversely, there tends to be more respect when colleagues know they can safely disagree. To make a difficult conversation safe, it is important to assume good intent. It keeps communication on the high road. Perhaps assumptions were made. You may have to go back and request context to gain a better understanding of the issue.

2. Participate as a learner and commit to hearing everyone's story.

In emotionally charged conversations, approaching the conversation with a learner's mindset is crucial. Each stakeholder should participate jointly in effective listening and problem solving. When participants feel as though they are heard, they are usually less resistant.

3. Stay calm.

High emotional intelligence is critical. Self-awareness is important. If you feel angry or defensive, you may ask yourself "What do I really want?" "How is what I am feeling affecting the way that I am responding?" This helps you to redirect to the rationale part of our brain. If someone is communicating with you in an angry manner, do not return the anger. View this as an opportunity to practice self-discipline and restraint. Show empathy. Remember that participants also face a lot of internal noise as they think about potential outcomes related to the conversation. This could affect rational thinking. They may have difficulty expressing their thoughts, so keep that in mind as you communicate with them.

4. Find common ground.

Finding common ground increases immediacy with the other part and helps to lead to mutually acceptable solutions.

5. Disagree diplomatically.

Difficult conversations involve different perspectives. You can disagree diplomatically by validating the views of others using I statements. To validate means you recognize their feelings as credible and legitimate. Statements should begin with, I think, I feel, or I believe …

6. Avoid exaggeration and either/or approaches.

Be mindful of using words such as always, never, most, or worst. Choosing words more accurately increases your credibility and helps to validate others. Approaching a difficult conversation with an "I'm right, you're wrong" approach usually doesn't end with a positive outcome.

7. Initiate the conversation, share stories, and focus on solutions.

Allow the other person to share first, and then tell your story to create a shared story.

Declare your intent to sincerely solve the problem.

Focus on solutions

Feedback is conversation that helps people to clarify, refine, and improve their practice. High-quality conversations can transform the learning culture. Conversations influence action. Actions lead to results.

STRATEGY #16

CELEBRATE SUCCESS

What do you have in place to recognize achievement in professional learning? If you want something to grow, you have to feed it. Celebrations are energizers that help participants leave with positive feelings regarding the training, since they are activities that recognize the work and effort of participants. They recognize those who have had "bright ideas," or those whom others have learned from in the session. Through celebration, learners have an opportunity to learn from each other, reflect, cross-pollinate ideas, and value one another.

Celebration activities allow participants to create mementos of their learning with manipulatives or easy-to-use craft objects.

An example of a celebration is having teachers taking pre-cut footprints and creating a mini-poster, titled "Steps to Student Engagement." Principals could create a card-stock bookmark with ways to leverage in-house resources.

Factors to consider are the resources available including time, space, and appropriateness.

What is a way that you can celebrate and leverage professional learning within your organization?

Final Thoughts

A professional learning leader can make or break an organization. High-quality professional learning can transform an organization. Our desire is that you will take the strategies learned within this book to make a positive difference for you and those you lead and teach. It is important to be the learning leader you would follow by maintaining high expectations, effectively communicating, and engaging in a cycle of continuous improvement. Just as we want teachers to have learner-centered classrooms, high-quality professional learning should also be learner-centered and results oriented. It would be great if you implemented everything gleaned from this book, but my request is that you choose just one strategy to implement with fidelity, and as you achieve success, implement others.

I wish you all of the benefits of empowerment and achievement!

REFERENCES

Acton, A. (2017, June 15). Innovator's challenge: Punch up your presentations and get off PowerPoint. Retrieved from https://www.forbes.com/sitcs/annabclacton/2017/06/15/innovators-challenge-punch-up-your-presentations-and-get-off-powerpoint/#60593ce14770

Avila, J. (2009). Professional learning communities. *Language Arts, 86*(4), 312–313.

Betof, E. (2009, July 27). Leaders as teachers. Retrieved from https://www.td.org/Publications/Newsletters/LX-Briefing/LXB-Archives/2009/07/Leaders-as-Teachers

Bitterman, T. (2010). *Teachers' perceptions of the impact of professional learning communities on teaching and learning in middle school science* (Doctoral dissertation). Available from ProQuest Dissertations and Theses database. (UMI No. 758398458)

Bowman, S. L. (2002). *Presenting with pizzazz: Terrific tips for topnotch trainers.* Glenbrook, NV: Bowperson Publishing.

Canfield, J., & Switzer, J. (2005). *The success principles: How to get from where you are to where you want to be.* New York: Harper Resource Book.

Carliner, S. (2012, September 20). How to evaluate informal learning. Retrieved May 15, 2016, from https://www.td.org/Publications/Newsletters/Links/2012/09/How-to-Evaluate-Informal-Learning

Carliner, S. (2014, September). 7 informal learning lessons. *Training, 51*(5), 30–33. Retrieved May 15, 2016, from Leadership & Management Learning Center.

Carter-Sackey, S. (2012). The 3 R's of learning time: Rethink, reshape, reclaim. *Journal of Staff Development, 33*(1), 46–48.

Conzemius, A., & Morganti-Fisher, T. (2012). *More than a SMART goal: Staying focused on student learning.* Bloomington, IN: Solution Tree Press.

Cross, J. (2007). *Informal learning: Rediscovering the natural pathways that inspire innovation and performance.* San Francisco: Pfeiffer/Wiley.

DuFour, R., & Eaker, R. E. (1998). *Professional learning communities at work: Best practices for enhancing student achievement.* Bloomington, IN: National Education Service.

DuFour, R. (2004). *Whatever it takes: How professional learning communities respond when kids don't learn.* Bloomington, IN: National Educational Service.

DuFour, R. (2006). *Learning by doing: A handbook for professional learning communities at work.* Bloomington, IN: Solution Tree.

DuFour, R. (2014). Harnessing the power of PLCs. *Educational Leadership, 71*(8), 30–35.

Easton, L. B. (2011). *Professional learning communities by design: Putting the learning back into PLCs.* Thousand Oaks, CA: Corwin.

Fink, L. D. (2003). *Creating significant learning experiences: An integrated approach to designing college courses.* San Francisco, CA: Jossey-Bass.

Fisher, D. P., & Frey, N. P. (2013). Implementing RTI in a high school: A case study. *Journal of Learning Disabilities, 46*(2), 99–114.

Floyd, K. (2011). *Interpersonal communication.* New York: McGraw-Hill.

Gordon, S. P. (2004). *Professional development for school improvement: Empowering learning communities.* Boston, MA: Allyn & Bacon.

Hamblin, H. T. (1917). *Dynamic thought.* Chicago, IL: Personality Institute.

Hamilton, C. (2014). *Communicating for results: A guide for business and the professions.* Boston, MA: Cengage Learning.

Hamilton, C. (2014). *Essentials of public speaking.* Belmont: Wadsworth Pub.

Hill, N. (1966). *Think and grow rich.* No. Hollywood, CA: Melvin Powers, Wilshire Book.

Hirsh, S., & Killion, J. (2007). *The learning educator: A new era for professional learning.* Oxford, OH: National Staff Development Council.

Hirsh, S., & Hord, S. (2012). *A playbook for professional learning: Putting standards into action.* Oxford, OH: Learning Forward.

Hord, S. M. (1997). *Professional learning communities: Communities of continuous inquiry and improvement.* Austin, TX: Southwest Educational Development Laboratory.

Jensen, E. (1998). *Sizzle & substance: Presenting with the brain in mind.* San Diego, CA: Brain Store.

Jones, L., Stall, G., & Yarbrough, D. (2013). The importance of professional learning communities for school improvement. *Creative Education, 4*(5), 357–361.

Killion, J., & Roy, P. (2009). *Becoming a learning school.* Oxford, OH: National Staff Development Council.

Kotter, J. P. (2012). *Leading change.* Boston, MA: Harvard Business Review Press.

Lucas, S. (2014). *The art of public speaking.* Boston, MA: McGraw Hill.

Meier, D. (2000). *The accelerated learning handbook: A creative guide to designing and delivering faster, more effective training programs.* New York: McGraw Hill.

Mizell, H., Hord, S., Killion, J., & Hirsh, S. (2011). New standards put the spotlight on professional learning. *Journal of Staff Development, 32*(4), 10–14.

Muir, G. (2013). *Instructional design that soars: Shaping what you know into classes that inspire.* Bothell, WA: Book Network.

Standards. (n.d.). Retrieved from http://learningforward.org/standards/

Peppers, G. J. (2014). *Teachers' perceptions and implementation of professional learning communities in a large suburban high school* (Master's thesis). Available from ProQuest Dissertations and Theses database. (UMI No. 1526306339)

Phillips, J. J., & Stone, R. D. (2002). *How to measure training results: A practical guide to tracking the six key indicators.* New York: McGraw-Hill.

Protheroe, N. (2008). *Teacher efficacy: What it is and does it matter?* Retrieved from http://www.naesp.org/resources/1/Principal/2008/M-Jp42.pdf

Rosenthal, R., & Babad, E. (1985). Pygmalian in the gymnasium. *Educational Leadership,* 36-39. Retrieved November 25, 2016.

Rosenthal, R., & Jacobson, L. (1968). *Pygmalion in the classroom: Teacher expectation and pupils' intellectual development.* New York: Holt, Rinehart and Winston.

Sellnow, D. D. (2005). *Confident public speaking.* Belmont, CA: Thomson/Wadsworth.

Senge, P. M. (1990). *The fifth discipline: The art and practice of the learning organization.* New York: Doubleday/Currency.

Shinn, F. S. (1925). *The game of life and how to play it.* Marina del Rey, CA: DeVorss.

Tate, M. L. (2004). *"Sit & get" won't grow dendrites: 20 professional learning strategies that engage the adult brain.* Thousand Oaks, CA: Corwin Press.

Tate, M. L. (2004). *"Sit & get" won't grow dendrites: 20 professional learning strategies that engage the adult brain.* Thousand Oaks, CA: Corwin Press.

Varela, A. M. (2012). Three major sins of professional development: How can we make it better? *Education Digest, 78*(4), 17–20. Available from ProQuest Dissertations and Theses database. (UMI No. 1197642568)

Wood, J. T. (2013). *Interpersonal communication: Everyday encounters.* Belmont, CA: Wadsworth Pub.

NOTES

NOTES

NOTES

Made in the USA
Lexington, KY
29 January 2018